Bicycles
on Parade

ACKNOWLEDGMENTS: The photographs are reproduced through the courtesy of: pp. 5, 36, 40, Julian Baum; pp. 6, 18, 21, 22, 24, 43, 44 (top), 45 (top), Smithsonian Institution; pp. 8, 15, The British Library; pp. 9, 17, 47 (top), Science Museum, London; pp. 10, 31, Radio Times Hulton Picture Library; pp. 11, 12, 27 (top), 34, 45 (bottom), British Crown Copyright, Science Museum, London; pp. 26, 27 (bottom), 44 (bottom), Schwinn Bicycle Company; p. 28, Photograph by Byron, The Byron Collection, Museum of the City of New York; p. 33, Motor Vehicle Manufacturers Association of the United States, Inc.; p. 39, Bicycle Manufacturers Association of America, Inc.; p. 41, Lorraine Rorke; p. 46 (top), Collection of Greenfield Village and the Henry Ford Museum, Dearborn, Michigan; p. 46 (bottom), Columbia Manufacturing Company; p. 47 (bottom), Richard Trombley and Gary Hansen; p. 50, The Library of Congress; pp. 53, 54, 55, Stan Pantovic.

Bicycles
on Parade

A BRIEF HISTORY

THOMAS F. PURSELL

Lerner Publications Company ▪ Minneapolis, Minnesota

to Geoffrey Thomas, future biker

LIBRARY OF CONGRESS CATALOGING IN PUBLICATION DATA

Pursell, Thomas F.
Bicycles on parade.

(Superwheels and Thrill Sports)
SUMMARY: Traces the history of the bicycle from the development of the French célérifère in the 1790's to 10-speed bikes of today.

1. Bicycles and tricycles—History—Juvenile literature. [1. Bicycles and bicycling—History] I. Title.

GV1040.5.P87   796.6'09   78-27403
ISBN 0-8225-0426-X

Manufactured in the United States of America. Published simultaneously in Canada by J. M. Dent & Sons (Canada) Ltd., Don Mills, Ontario.

International Standard Book Number: 0-8225-0426-X
Library of Congress Catalog Card Number: 78-27403

1 2 3 4 5 6 7 8 9 10 85 84 83 82 81 80

CONTENTS

INTRODUCTION

Whirring along on ten-speed bikes, modern bicyclists may not think about the history of their machines. They may not know that the mechanical ancestor of the ten-speed bike was a contraption called the Hobby-horse. Or that bicycles were once as tall as people! This book tells the story of bicycles old and new. It explains how bikes have helped to make our modern world what it is today. And it peeks into the future to see what the bicycles of tomorrow might be like.

Our story begins hundreds of years ago and thousands of miles away, in England and France. There, the colorful history of the bicycle unfolds—a history as bumpy as the long-ago roads of Europe.

This clumsy-looking machine, with its heavy wooden wheels and frame, was one of the world's first bicycles.

THE HOBBY-HORSE

It is hard to say who invented the first bicycle. In an English church built in 1642, a stained-glass window shows a young musician sitting on a two-wheeled machine. Yet that window remains a mystery. No one knows whether the artist who made it just imagined the two-wheeled contraption or whether he actually saw one.

Most historians agree that a young Frenchman, the Count de Sivrac, made the first bicycle. In the year 1791, he amazed passersby in a Paris park by scooting around on a thing he called a *célérifère* (say·lair·eh·fuhr). Onlookers were so surprised and amused that they began to clap and cheer.

The *célérifère*—later called the Hobbyhorse—was really just a wooden frame with wooden wheels attached at either end. This first bicycle had no pedals. Riders traveled along by pushing off the ground with their feet and coasting between pushes. They were truly "running" their machines!

Riding the *célérifère* may have been fun, but it was also hard work. Controlling the machine was difficult. Since the front wheel did not move from side to side, the *célérifère* could not be steered. In order to turn, riders either had to lean to one side, which didn't work very well, or they had to pick up the whole machine and point it where they

wanted to go. The Count de Sivrac's invention was, in fact, a very heavy, clumsy machine that was used mostly by strong young men. History's first bicycle had so many disadvantages that it is not surprising that people soon lost interest in it.

For years, nothing was done with the Hobby-horse, and the idea nearly died. In 1817, however, a German inventor gave the Hobby-horse new life. Baron Karl von Drais liked tinkering with machinery and inventing

gadgets much better than he liked his job. As the chief forester for a grand duke, he spent most of his days walking over miles of mountain trails and forest paths. It was only natural, then, that he invented something to help him get done with his work and get back to his hobby. What von Drais did was to mount the front wheel of his Hobby-horse in a socket on the frame, so that the wheel could swivel from side to side. He then attached a handlebar to the front wheel. By

An early English Hobby-horse

moving the handlebar, he could now turn the front wheel as well. Von Drais had made a Hobby-horse that he could steer!

In 1818 von Drais took his new invention to Paris and showed it off. Soon the new Hobby-horse design gained popularity and spread to other countries. The Hobby-horse caught on especially well in England. Wealthy young men called "dandies" raced their machines around London at the fantastic speed of nine miles per hour. Even stylish young ladies were caught up in the fad, somehow managing to ride in their long skirts and fancy bonnets.

All the excitement over the Hobby-horse amused some people but annoyed others. Many people thought that the young riders looked ridiculous on their "dandy-horses." Newspapers and cartoonists began to make fun of the new machines and of the people who rode them. The English poet John Keats called bicycling "the nothing of the day."

Because Hobby-horses had no pedals and were hard to steer, they were very difficult to ride.

In fact, the Hobby-horse *was* awkward and impractical. The machines were heavy, hard to steer, and so expensive that only the wealthy could afford them. And since Hobby-horses had no pedals, their riders had to get off and walk the machines up even the gentlest of hills. By 1820, it was becoming very unfashionable to ride a Hobby-horse. In England, as well as in other countries, bicycles nearly disappeared for over 40 years.

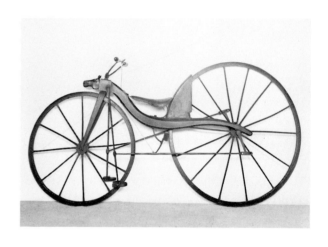

Kirkpatrick Macmillan built only one rear-driven Hobby-horse. This is a replica of his cycle.

But the bicycle was not forgotten. It was only waiting for someone to improve it. Many people tried. The most important of these inventors was a Scottish blacksmith named Kirkpatrick Macmillan. In 1839, Macmillan got the bright idea of attaching a system of levers, called treadles, to the rear wheel of a Hobby-horse. When the blacksmith pushed the treadles with his feet, they turned the rear wheel of the machine, propelling it forward. Unlike earlier Hobby-horse designs, Macmillan's bicycle moved by mechanical power, not just by leg power.

Macmillan soon became famous in his hometown of Courthill, where he pedaled about the countryside at speeds up to 14 miles per hour. In 1842, the Scotsman became the first person to get a ticket for riding a bicycle! He knocked over a pedestrian in Glasgow and was fined five shillings.

Unfortunately, Macmillan's fame was short-lived. Kirkpatrick Macmillan made only one Hobby-horse, and he didn't sell his idea to anyone else. In the history of the bicycle, the Macmillan machine was a brilliant dead end.

THE BONESHAKER

In 1861, a Paris businessman took his old Hobby-horse to the shops of Pierre Michaux, a coach repairman. The businessman wanted his machine fixed. Pierre Michaux did more than fix the old Hobby-horse; he made history with it!

At first, Michaux and his sons Henry and Ernest stood looking at the broken-down Hobby-horse, wondering where to begin. Suddenly, the older man had a brilliant idea. He thought of another wheeled machine—a grindstone. A grindstone, like a bicycle wheel, is mounted so that it can spin. But a grindstone is turned by cranks. Thinking aloud, Michaux suggested putting such cranks on a Hobby-horse, cranks that riders could turn with their feet. His son Ernest did the

An English Boneshaker

experiment, and a new kind of bicycle was born. This is the machine that history usually calls the Velocipede (veh•LOSS•uh•*peed*), or the Boneshaker.

Boneshakers usually had brightly painted wrought-iron frames instead of the old-style wooden ones. Nuts, bolts, pedals, and other hardware were made of highly polished brass. Wheels were made of wood and protected by inch-wide iron tires. Because these materials had to be put together by hand, even the simplest models were costly. The least expensive Boneshakers sold for 75 dollars, while the best models cost up to 160 dollars.

The history of the Boneshaker is different from country to country. In the United States, Boneshakers became a craze in 1869.

Books were written about the sport of bicycling, and many carriage-makers turned to making Boneshakers. But—just as happened with the Hobby-horse in England 50 years before—the craze in America suddenly died. In fact, it lasted barely a year! By late 1869, so few people wanted Boneshakers that desperate makers were selling their machines for as little as 12 dollars.

Why did the Boneshaker fad die so suddenly in America? The reasons are not clear. Certainly the machines were uncomfortable. They jolted and jarred their riders, who had to pedal from an awkward position. Leaning back and straining at the pedals, riders might have called their cycles "backbreakers" as well as Boneshakers!

Probably the main reason for the Boneshaker's failure in America, however, was that people were simply not ready to accept the odd foreign invention. To most people, Boneshakers seemed both dangerous and impractical. Soon laws were passed to prohibit riding the machines on sidewalks and in parks. With nowhere to ride but muddy, rut-filled roads, most American cyclists gave up in disgust.

In France, meanwhile, Pierre Michaux and others were improving the original Boneshaker design. Their improvements made the Boneshaker—which by 1869 was being called the bicycle—safer, lighter, and faster. For years, France led the world in bicycle technology. In 1870, however, French bicycle development came to an abrupt halt. That year, war broke out between France and the German state of Prussia. The Franco-Prussian War of 1870-71 occupied all of France's industry, leaving little time or money for making something as frivolous as bicycles. The war ended in a horrible defeat for France, and the French cycle industry never completely recovered.

In England, the Boneshaker met with lasting success. In 1869, a young man named Rowley Turner introduced the French Boneshaker to England. Turner astonished the crowd in a London gymnasium by pedaling around the room without once touching his feet to the floor. Remembering the Hobby-horse, people in those days thought that a person could not balance on two wheels without touching the ground at least once in a while. Turner and his Boneshaker proved them wrong.

Boneshakers became extremely popular in the United States. In New York City alone, 10,000 men enrolled in Velocipede riding schools like the one shown here.

After making a splash in London, Turner took his machine to Coventry, England. There, he persuaded the Coventry Sewing Machine Company to begin making Boneshakers. Until cycling caught on in England, Turner argued, the machines could be sold in France, where bicycling was already the rage. Within a short time, several other companies in Coventry also began making bicycles. By the 1870s, Coventry had become the bicycle-manufacturing capital of the world.

When France went to war in 1870, the bicycle companies of Coventry began to sell more machines to their own countrymen. That was not hard to do, since the English were already falling in love with the new machines. A number of improvements further encouraged the growth of the sport.

One improvement was the wire-spoked wheel. Wire wheels were lighter than wooden ones, and they had more give when they hit rocks or holes in the road. People also reduced the weight of their machines by building bikes with frames made of iron tubes instead of solid wrought iron. Lighter weight was an important feature to the average rider, as well as to those who were interested in racing.

Another improvement came from abroad. In 1868, the Hanlon brothers of New York suggested putting rubber strips on the wheels of bicycles. The rubber tires gave a softer ride than the iron-rimmed wheels that were then in use. They also stuck to the road better, making bicycling safer. Before rubber tires were invented, riders never knew when they might be thrown off their bikes because their iron tires had lost their grip on the road.

Perhaps the most important change in the bicycle, however, had to do with the size of the wheels. The original Hobby-horse had front and back wheels that were the same size. Little by little, however, the front wheels of some Boneshakers were made larger and larger. The reason for the change to larger front wheels is easy to understand. Bicycle pedals were fixed to the center, or hub, of the front wheel. One turn of the

The Hanlon brothers improved the velocipede by adding rubber tires.

pedals made one full turn of the front wheel. For example, if the outside of the front wheel measured 90 inches, one full turn of the pedals would move the bicycle exactly that far—90 inches. The larger the front wheel was made, the farther a bike would move with one turn of the pedals.

For the rider, a large front wheel was harder to turn at first. But once the bike was moving, it could easily outrace a smaller machine. By 1870, the front wheels of bicycles were often 12 inches larger in diameter than the rear wheels. Soon they would get even bigger.

THE ORDINARY

In 1871, a new kind of bicycle appeared in England. Its inventor, James Starley of Coventry, called it the Ariel. The Ariel had a giant front wheel and a tiny back one. Despite its extraordinary proportions, this bicycle style was so popular that it soon became known simply as the "Ordinary" bicycle. In fact, by the mid-1870s, almost no other kind of bicycle was being made. Because of the Ariel and his other cycle inventions, James Starley became known as the "Father of the Cycling Industry."

The Ordinary had many advantages over the Boneshaker. Of course, the biggest advantage was that huge front wheel! With front wheels up to 60 inches across, Ordinaries could travel at speeds of 15 miles per hour and more. The rear wheels were tiny by comparison. They usually measured only 16 to 18 inches across. The great difference in size between the front and rear wheels reminded some people of two English coins, the large penny and the much smaller farthing. Laughingly, the English referred to high-wheelers as "Penny-farthings." Even today, that name is often used to describe these machines.

Another advantage of the Ordinary bicycle was that it was more comfortable than earlier designs. Riders no longer had to pedal from a back-breaking position. Because the seats of Ordinaries were positioned more nearly over the pedals, riders were able to use their weight to help turn the pedals. Now the bicycle was getting somewhere!

This improved design worked so well that

it renewed the popularity of bicycling in the United States. The sport had been practically dead in America since the passing of the Boneshaker in 1869. But in 1876, a shipment of British high-wheelers was shown at the Centennial Exhibition in Philadelphia. Americans loved the new bikes. In 1877, Colonel Albert A. Pope of Boston began to import Ordinaries. One year later, he started producing his famous Columbia-brand bicycles.

One of Pope's Ordinaries—the Columbia Light Roadster made in 1886—was typical of the new design. The Light Roadster was available in seven different front-wheel sizes, ranging from 47 to 59 inches. There were two rear-wheel sizes, 16 and 18 inches.

The wheels had steel wire spokes and were driven by adjustable pedals attached to a ball-bearing axle. The frame and handlebars were made of steel tubing. The seat was leather, and the tires were solid rubber. The 1886 Light Roadster sold for about 135 dollars. That made it too expensive for most people to buy new. Most workers and tradespeople, however, were able to purchase such high-wheelers second-hand. Many of these people cherished their machines and rode them well into the 20th century.

In its day, the Ordinary was fashionable and elegant, especially for young men. Pedaling along at 15 miles per hour, the rider of an Ordinary thought himself the highest of sportsmen. With his head fully seven or eight

The Columbia Light Roadster

feet off the ground, he *was* the highest of sportsmen, or at least the tallest. From such an elevated perch, cyclists sped down country roads, peering over the tops of hedges and seeing things that mere walkers could not possibly see.

If cyclists looked down on other people, though, there were many who did not "look up" to them. Some people thought a grown man sitting on a wheel looked like a fool.

"Monkey on a wire!" they shouted. Newspapers and magazines did not make as much fun of the Ordinary as they had of the Hobbyhorse before it. But they reported every bloody detail of bicycle accidents, exaggerating the dangers of riding.

Cycling enthusiasts, on the other hand, were eager to show that the bicycle was here to stay. To prove their machines—and their skill as riders—people began taking remarkable trips on their Ordinary bicycles. The greatest was a trip around the world taken by an American reporter, Thomas Stevens. Beginning in San Francisco in April 1884, Stevens rode his American-made Columbia bicycle across the United States in 103½ days. He then loaded his bike on a ship,

Racing the Ordinary became a popular new sport in the 1880s.

crossed the Atlantic Ocean, and continued riding across Europe and Asia. Stevens struggled up mountains and through jungles. He even outraced bandits on horseback! The young reporter returned to San Francisco, coming from the opposite direction, in December 1886. His round-the-world journey had taken 32 months.

Such adventures did little to change the minds of those who objected to bicycles. In some ways, the critics were right: the Ordinary *did* pose serious problems for the rider. For one thing, the bicycle was so high that even experienced riders had trouble getting on and off it. There were three usual methods of mounting a high-wheeler. The rider could hop along behind the machine, resting one foot on the rear step. When he had enough speed, he swung himself into the seat. This "hopping" method was anything but dignified. In the "jumping" method, the rider ran alongside his machine. He then tried to catch one of the pedals on its way around and to leap into the saddle. If the rider's timing wasn't perfect, however, he took a nasty spill.

The last method of mounting an Ordinary seems to be the most logical. The rider leaned his machine against the side of a building, or he had someone hold the bike up while he mounted it. This way, of course, was not very adventuresome, but it probably prevented a lot of bruises and bad language. Getting off an Ordinary was also a problem. To dismount, the rider had to reverse one of the mounting methods—or come down with a crash.

Getting on and off an Ordinary was difficult; but the greatest hazard of all was that of falling while riding. On an Ordinary, the rider sat on top of the huge front wheel. To pedal hard, he had to lean forward over the wheel. This put his balance, or center of gravity, too far forward, so that a pebble in the road could make even an experienced rider tumble headfirst over the handlebars. Cyclists had names for this kind of fall. They called it the "noseover," the "header," or the "imperial crowner." On a modern bicycle—even a child's model—such a fall can be serious. On a 60-inch Ordinary, it could be fatal!

Cycling tours were also a popular pastime. This 1879 photograph shows a men's riding club in Massachusetts.

The dangers of riding an Ordinary kept many people from bicycling at all. Women at that time were not encouraged to engage in hard or dangerous activities. Although a few daring women experimented with Ordinaries, most looked for other forms of recreation and transportation. Likewise, older people did not feel safe on high-wheelers. Because of these and other drawbacks, inventors began to work on a better design— a different kind of bicycle that *everyone* could ride.

THE SAFETY BICYCLE

Almost as soon as the first Ordinary bicycle arrived on the scene, people began demanding a safer machine. At first, any design for a safer bicycle was called a "Safety."

The earliest Safety bicycle was the Safety Ordinary. This design still had a high front wheel, but the seat was mounted farther back on the frame. The pedals, no longer attached to the hub of the front wheel, were hooked up to levers or chains to drive the wheel. Now cyclists were able to ride their machines from a safer, yet comfortable, position.

Another kind of early Safety looked like a backward Ordinary. This model—called the Star—had a high wheel in the *rear* and a small one in *front*. The idea, of course, was to move the center of gravity back, so that the rider would no longer fall forward. Some people joked that the problem had only been reversed: now, they said, riders would fall over backward!

Although the new high-wheeled Safeties were an improvement over the original

Ordinaries, they were still not safe enough. The first true Safety bicycle was made by H. J. Lawson in 1879. Lawson called his design the "Bicyclette." The Bicyclette had a 40-inch front wheel and a 24-inch rear wheel. These smaller wheels made the Bicyclette lower than the Ordinary, so that riders didn't have as far to fall. A more important feature of Lawson's bicycle was the chain-driven rear wheel. Chains had been used before to drive the front wheel of the Ordinary, but never before had the now-familiar sprocket, pedals, and chain been used to drive the rear wheel. It was this design that eventually became what we now call a Safety bicycle. Few people, however, liked Lawson's strange new design, and the Bicyclette never caught on.

Early Safety bicycles included the Star High Safety *(above)*, **the Lawson Bicyclette** *(page 27, top),* **and the Rover Safety** *(page 27, bottom).*

In 1884 John K. Starley, James Starley's nephew, made the first popular line of Safety bicycles. Starley's machine, called the "Rover," succeeded where the Bicyclette had failed. But not even this design was an overnight success. Riders of the elegant old high-wheelers considered Safety bicycles to be unstylish and even ugly. They complained that the new, smaller bikes splashed mud on riders and let dogs snap at their heels. Besides, Ordinaries could easily outdistance the first smaller-wheeled Safety machines. Despite these objections, however, Safeties steadily gained popularity and soon replaced the high-wheelers.

Why did Safety bicycles replace Ordinaries? The Safety had two great mechanical

This bicyclist was a prize winner in a cycle parade in New York City in 1898.

advantages over the high-wheeled Ordinary. First, the Safety was made with a chain-and-sprocket rear-wheel drive. This meant that the front wheel no longer had pedals on it. Instead, the pedals were attached to a sprocket directly beneath the seat. Before, with pedals attached to the front axle, the front wheel swerved back and forth as the rider pushed first on one pedal, then on the other. A rear-wheel-driven bicycle, then, was easier to steer and gave a steadier ride.

A second advantage of the Safety also had to do with the chain-and-sprocket drive. That system gave the rider mechanical help in driving the cycle. Here is how it works. The pedals of a Safety are fixed to a large toothed wheel called the sprocket. A chain fits over the teeth of the sprocket and connects it to a smaller toothed wheel on the rear axle. Toothed wheels of this sort are called *gears*. As the rider turns the pedals and sprocket of a Safety, the chain sends, or transmits, the power of the rider's legs back to the rear wheel, through the smaller gear. Now think—if a large gear and a smaller gear are linked together in this way, which one will turn faster? If you think the smaller one, you are right! The smaller gear turns much faster than the sprocket and pedals, and it makes the driving wheel go around just as fast. The gears of the chain-and-sprocket drive make the driving wheel go around *more than once* for each turn of the pedals. Fitting a Safety cycle with gears in this mechanical way of giving it a very large driving wheel, like an Ordinary has.

One problem with the gear system, however, is that a "mechanically large" driving wheel is still harder to turn than a small wheel. Inventors solved that problem by fitting cycles with adjustable gears. Adjustable gears dated back to James Starley's early cycles, but it was not until well into the time of the Safety that they became practical. With adjustable gears, cyclists can choose, in a mechanical way, the size of their driving wheel. "Small-wheel" gearings, which are easy to turn, are for slow speeds and steep hills. "Large-wheel" gearings are hard to turn at first, but are good for high speeds on level roads. Adjustable gears gave Safeties all the advantages of high-wheelers without the disadvantages.

The Safety bicycle's main advantage, however, was just what its name suggested. It was much *safer* than the Ordinary. The new machines were lower; so riders did not have as far to fall. The rider's center of gravity was safely over the middle of the bicycle—not over the front wheel. No more would riders be thrown on their heads because of a pebble in the road. Now anyone could ride a bicycle. And almost everyone did!

The peak of the cycle boom came in the 1890s. By then, everybody seemed to be bicycling, and millions of machines were being produced each year. One of the reasons for this great popularity was that bicycles

During the 1890s, many women took to the roads on their Safety bicycles.

were becoming much less expensive. In 1899, for example, the Mead Cycle Company of Chicago sold its models for as little as 7 to 12 dollars. That was a far cry from the 313 dollars that the Columbia Ordinary had cost 20 years before.

With bicycles so inexpensive, reliable, and safe, things couldn't have looked better for the cycle industry. To manufacturers and cyclists alike, the bicycle must have seemed like the greatest invention in history. Did cycling enthusiasts ever suspect that the road was once more going to get bumpy for the bicycle? That very soon a noisy, smelly, unreliable four-wheeled contraption was about to challenge the two-wheeler—and change the world?

THE MODERN BICYCLE

To tell the story of the modern bicycle, it is also necessary to tell a little bit about that four-wheeled machine, the automobile. Where did these "horseless carriages" come from? We think of the automobile as being a much newer invention than the bicycle. Actually, it is older. In 1769, fully 22 years before the Count de Sivrac invented the Hobby-horse, a Frenchman named Nicolas Joseph Cugnot built the first automobile. Cugnot's automobile was a steam-powered, four-wheeled carriage used by the French army. It was a strange-looking machine with a top speed of only two miles per hour. Even the Hobby-horse was faster than that!

For more than 100 years, machines like Cugnot's were rare curiosities, impractical for everyday use. It was not until the early 20th century that automobiles really caught on as a means of transportation. American inventors like Henry Ford, Charles Duryea, and Albert A. Pope—all men who had worked on bicycles earlier—were mainly responsible for the automobile's success. Horseless carriages, they believed, could do anything bicycles could do—and do it better.

The automobile affected bicycling differently around the world. In Europe and other parts of the world, most people could not afford cars. There, bicycles remained the most important form of personal transportation. In the prosperous United States, however, things were different. After 1900, automobiles got cheaper, faster, and more

After 1900, more people were purchasing automobiles, and auto races replaced cycling events in popularity. This Franklin was featured in a 1904 race in New York City.

reliable. Many people who would have bought bicycles before bought cars now instead. The bicycle business fell off sharply. Business was so bad that between 1900 and 1905, two out of three cycle companies went out of operation. By 1905, people in America began thinking of the bicycle as nothing more than a toy. It was something for children to get around on until they were old enough to drive. The country that had been in love with the bicycle was now in love with the automobile.

In the 1950s, Alexander Moulton designed the first new bicycle in more than 50 years. This is the MK3 model.

Inventors also lost interest in the bicycle. In fact, there were no really new bicycle designs until the late 1950s. It was then that an Englishman named Alexander Moulton introduced his small-wheeled machines. The Moulton cycles usually had simple, lightweight frames, long seats, rubber suspensions, and wheels measuring only 18 to 20 inches across. The cycles performed far beyond their size, however. Fitted with extras like five-speed gears, the new small-wheelers were able to keep up with larger machines, even over long distances. The Moulton bicycle started the fad for small-wheeled "novelty" bikes, which are still popular today.

About the same time that Alexander Moulton was making his first bicycles in England, something very important was happening across the ocean: Americans were rediscovering the bicycle. There were many reasons for this rediscovery. One was the nation's new president, John F. Kennedy, who was elected in 1960. This dynamic young leader encouraged Americans to do things with "vigor," and he emphasized the need for physical fitness. Slowly at first, then in greater and greater numbers, Americans began cycling to get in shape. In fact, doctors found that cycling is one of the best forms of exercise, because it uses the whole body. Only swimming and jogging are more beneficial than bicycling.

People turned to cycling for other reasons, too. Through the 1960s and 1970s, inflation made automobiles more expensive than ever—too expensive for some people. Gasoline prices also rose as the energy crisis hit and as oil became scarcer and scarcer. Automobiles, to many people, were becoming more trouble than they were worth. Bicycles, on the other hand, cost little to buy and required nothing but some healthy exercise to run.

Anyone who has ever choked on exhaust fumes or resented the roar of traffic knows another reason why bicycles have become more popular in recent years. Bicycles don't pollute the environment as cars do. During the 1960s, automobile pollution was recognized as a serious threat to the quality of modern life. It was then that people began to think twice about what the automobile was doing to the world. Many of these doubters turned to bicycles for transportation. To them, bicycling was somehow simpler and more natural than riding in a car. On a bike one sees more, hears more, *feels* more of one's surroundings than in an automobile. Bicycling protects the environment and makes people feel more a part of it as well.

Cycle technology has also added to the new popularity of bicycling. Bicycles today are better in every way than they were 100

or even 50 years ago. Modern cycles are comfortable and safe. They are available in a host of shapes and sizes to suit every rider. Cycles have truly come a long way since the clumsy Hobby-horse. One thing has not changed, however: cycling is as much fun today as it ever was, and that is the best reason of all for riding a bike.

As bicycling has flourished in recent years, so has the cycle industry. Sales have soared, and manufacturers have begun experimenting with new models. The result can be seen in the wide variety of cycles on the market today. Looking through a modern bike shop—or even at a bike rack outside a school or an office building—one might think there are a hundred different kinds of bicycles. Nearly all of them, however, are of five main types.

The Heavyweights. First there is the heavyweight, or heavy-duty bicycle. This is the kind of machine that most resembles the original Safety bike. These cycles have wide touring seats, strong steel frames, and level handlebars. Their wheels are generally 24 or 26 inches across and have wide balloon tires. Fenders over the wheels protect the rider from mud and water. Heavyweights usually have only one gear speed and use coaster brakes.

Some people consider heavyweights to be old-fashioned, but they are still the best machines for people who use their cycles roughly. Their strength and wide tires also make them the most suitable machines to learn on. Nevertheless, these bikes do have certain disadvantages. With their weight and single gear speed, heavyweights are not good machines for long trips.

The Middleweights. A second class of bicycle can be called the middleweight, or all-purpose bike. Sometimes called English racers, they are not really racing machines at all. Like the heavyweights, the middleweights have touring seats, fenders, level handlebars, and 24- and 26-inch wheels. As their name suggests, however, middleweights are lighter than heavyweights. They have narrower wheels and three- to ten-speed gears. These machines also feature brakes on both the front and rear wheels. The rider applies them by squeezing levers mounted on the handlebars.

Because middleweight bikes have some of the advantages of both the heavyweights and the more expensive machines, they truly deserve the name of "all-purpose" bicycles. They are good for just riding around town as well as for longer trips in the country.

A small-wheeler

A middleweight bicycle

A ten-speed bicycle

A heavyweight bicycle

Ten-speeds are the best bicycles for long-distance riding.

Ten-speeds. A third type of bicycle is the ten-speed, or lightweight. Ten-speeds have small, hard saddles; lowered handlebars; thin, hard tires; and ten-speed gears. Like middleweights, they have brakes on both the front and rear wheels, which are usually 26 inches in diameter. But ten-speeds lack fenders and, of course, are even lighter than the middleweights. Ten-speeds are the best machines for long-distance riding. They can be complicated and fragile, however, and require much care. Ten-speeds are fine, expensive machines, not built for stunt-riding or bumping over curbs.

Small-wheelers. Small-wheelers make up a fourth class of bicycle. These bikes have wheels that are usually only 20 inches across. Small-wheelers also feature high-rise handle-

Small-wheelers are good for stunt riding. With five-speed transmissions, they can also be used for touring.

bars, long banana seats, and rubber suspensions. They sometimes have three- or five-speed stick shifts, disc brakes, and other automobile-type accessories. Because these cycles are often made to look as much as possible like motorcycles or automobiles, they are sometimes called "novelty" bikes. Such dressed-up machines appeal to young people who love cars and motorcycles but are not yet old enough to drive.

Racing Cycles. Finally, there are the racing bicycles, which are in a class by themselves. Their frames, wheels, handlebars, and saddles resemble those of the ten-speed bikes. But racers are stripped of all unnecessary equipment. They usually have no brakes, only one gear speed, and may weigh less than half as much as other cycles. Built to be as light and fast as possible, racing bikes are good only for racing.

Racing cycles are very light and are designed for speed.

A LOOK AT SOME OTHER CYCLES

Although most people today associate cycling with *bi*cycles, this wasn't always so. Inventors have experimented with many other kinds of cycles over the years. Some of them are still around today; others have been all but forgotten. Each, however, deserves at least a small place in the story of cycling.

One-wheelers. The simplest kind of cycle to be invented was the *unicycle*. It had no handlebars, brakes, or gears—just a seat and frame mounted on a single wheel. Needless to say, the unicycle was never meant to be a serious form of transportation. Rather, it was designed as a stunt machine to be used by trick riders and acrobats. It is still used this way today, which explains why you are more likely to see a unicycle in a circus than in a bike shop.

Another kind of one-wheeled machine was called the *monocycle*. The monocycle had a seat mounted on swivels *inside* an enormous wheel. One such machine was the Greene and Dyer Monocycle, made in 1869. The rider of this monocycle ran the huge, eight-foot-high wheel by cranks and treadles, but the contraption did not work very well. The inventors gave up on their machine when it crashed the first time on the road. Other monocycles suffered similar fates.

The Dicycle. The bicycle was not the only two-wheeled cycle to be invented. Around 1880, E. C. T. Otto patented the Otto Dicycle. This machine had two wheels mounted side by side. The rider sat on a saddle between the wheels and tried very hard to keep from tipping over frontwards or backwards. Dicycles enjoyed a brief popularity.

A monocycle

The B. S. A. Company of England actually made about one thousand of these odd cycles before people finally gave up on them.

The Tricycle. A more successful machine was the tricycle. For a long while, in fact, the tricycle was nearly as popular as its two-wheeled cousin. The reason for the development of the tricycle is easy to understand. With three wheels, the tricycle did not require the rider to balance. Many people who were afraid of bicycling enjoyed tricycling.

Like bicycles, tricycles went through many stages of development. Some early tricycles had two small wheels in tandem and one very large driving wheel off to the side. Others had two large wheels in front and one small one behind. Finally, in the 1880s, tricycles began to look the way they do today, with

An early tricycle

one large wheel in front and two smaller ones behind.

Today, tricycles are gaining new popularity. The current cycle boom still finds many people who do not feel confident on two wheels. These people are turning once again to the stable, sturdy three-wheeler.

Quadricycles and Pentacycles. If a cycle can have two or three wheels, why not four or five? Inventors *did* experiment with "quadricycles" and "pentacycles." Such machines were mainly used by mail carriers and tradespeople who needed to carry heavy loads. Quadricycles and pentacycles were complicated and rather clumsy, however. They never became very popular.

An 1895 duplex tricycle for two riders

A duplex quadricycle, or four-wheeled cycle

An 1851 quadricycle

Sociables and Tandems. Other kinds of cycles had more than one rider! Machines called "sociables" were designed so that two riders could pedal side by side. Some sociables had two wheels, others three or four. Even the ones with four wheels, however, were difficult to balance and to steer. Sociables soon gave way to a better kind of two-rider machine.

The two-rider bicycle that we know today is called the tandem. The tandem was first built in the mid-1880s in England. The tandem had a traditional bicycle design, with the riders sitting one behind the other. This arrangement was faster and more stable than the sociable design.

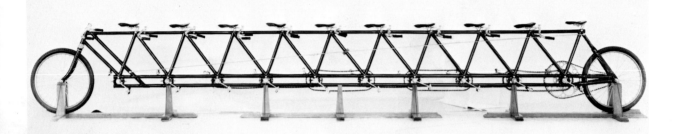

This unusual bicycle is an early-model tandem for 10 riders. Below is a modern five-speed tandem.

Today, many cycle companies make tandem bicycles. Some of these bikes have ten-speed gears, lowered handlebars, and other features found on expensive lightweight cycles. And today it is as much fun as ever to ride with a friend on a bicycle built for two.

Motorcycles. Another kind of cycle moves under its own power. An early example of this kind of vehicle, the Roper Steam Velocipede, was built in 1869. This contraption

A model of the motorcycle built by Gottlieb Daimler in 1885. This machine was the forerunner of today's motorcycles, including the middleweight bike below.

looked like a regular Boneshaker, but it featured a steam boiler underneath the seat. This steampowered Boneshaker was an ancestor of the modern motorcycle!

Other self-propelled cycles were built in the 19th century. Most of them started with bicycle designs. In the middle of the 1880s, an American named Lucius D. Copeland put a steam engine on a Star bicycle. At about the same time in Germany, Gottlieb Daimler mounted a newfangled gasoline engine on a bicycle, and the first true motorcycle was born.

A look at these early motorcycles reminds one that the bicycle and the motorcycle share a common history. Even the fanciest modern "chopper" is related to the humble Hobby-horse.

THE BICYCLE AND THE MODERN WORLD

Over the years, people have changed and improved bicycles a great deal. Few people stop to think, however, that bicycles have also changed people! In fact, they have changed the world we live in. How, one might ask, could a simple machine do that?

First of all, people needed the bicycle, or something like it. From the beginning of time, people have needed transportation—a way to get from one place to another. At first, of course, people walked. Later, they rode horses, camels, oxen, or other animals. Where there was water, people used boats. Finally, people invented iron horses—railroads—to carry them where they wanted to go. But each of these forms of transportation had disadvantages. Walking was slow and tiring.

Boats and trains could not go everywhere, and they were expensive. Horses, too, were inconvenient. They cost a lot to buy and feed, and they required a lot of care and attention.

Bicycles, on the other hand, were faster and less tiring than walking. By the 1890s, they were also becoming inexpensive. And unlike horses, they could be kept in the front hall. Bicycles filled the need people had always had for personal transportation. With a bicycle, a man or woman could speed 10 miles to work in less than an hour. A housewife could go to market in a few hours instead of taking a whole day. Children who lived far from a school could ride their bikes to class. Bicycles made life easier for millions of people everywhere.

The bicycle not only gave people a practical form of transportation. It also gave them an inexpensive way to travel—just for the fun of it! Not too long ago, the average person's world was very small. Not many people were able to journey more than a few miles from where they were born. The bicycle let all kinds of people get out and see the world. At last people could satisfy their curiosity about what lay over the next hill. The bicycle made people want to travel.

The new freedom that bicycles gave people especially changed the lives of women. In the 1890s, women were expected to stay at home. They were not encouraged to travel or to do things on their own. With the invention of the Safety bicycle, however, things began to change. Women seized the opportunity that bicycles gave them for a more independent style of life. Soon women were pedaling off to work, to visit friends, or were riding just for the sport. With so many women cycling—even racing—it was plain that females were not the "weak" creatures that men had thought them to be.

The bicycle also helped to change women's fashions. In the early days of cycling, women had to wear long skirts and petticoats, which were often made of wool. These garments were anything but comfortable for vigorous sport! Soon, some women began to wear more practical styles such as bloomers, which allowed them more freedom of movement.

In the 1890s, women's lifestyles and fashions were greatly influenced by the growing popularity of the bicycle.

By the turn of the century, there was a full-scale revolution going on in women's fashions, and the bicycle was largely responsible for it.

Bicycles had an effect on technology as well as on people's everyday lives. For one thing, bicycle shops were training grounds for inventors of the future. Many pioneers of the automobile, men like Colonel Albert A. Pope, Charles Duryea, and George Pierce, made bicycles first. Working with cycles, they learned the skills that led them to develop their lines of automobiles and motorcycles.

Two other famous inventors started their careers as bicycle mechanics. Orville and Wilbur Wright had a bicycle shop in Dayton, Ohio. There, they became interested in flying machines. Their interest led them to Kitty Hawk, North Carolina, where in 1903 they made history by flying the first airplane. Who knows whether the Wright brothers would have invented the airplane had they not been interested in bicycles first.

Today, in the age of computers and spaceships, the bicycle seems like a simple machine. We take it completely for granted. Henry Ford didn't, though; nor did the Wright brothers. They realized, perhaps more clearly than we can, that the bicycle is a vital link in the chain of mechanical and scientific progress; a chain that has already led to the moon and that will someday go beyond.

THE FUTURE OF THE BICYCLE

We have seen what some of the bicycles of the past were like. From the Hobby-horse to the ten-speed, bicycles have come a long way. What's next? one might ask. What will bicycles be like in the future? Here are a few possibilities.

Some inventors say that thin shells of clear plastic will cover the cycles of the future. These shells would be streamlined to reduce wind resistance, thus making cycles faster. Shells like these are already being tested on experimental bicycles and motorcycles.

In the years ahead, cycle seats might also change. If riders were sitting back in bucket-type seats, they could use their backs as well as their legs to push harder on the pedals. This position would make cycles faster and, perhaps, more comfortable, too. Cycles with bucket seats and plastic shells might well be used as passenger vehicles.

Perhaps the wave of the future will not be bicycles at all. It may be tricycles or even quadricycles. Such machines could have two or more seats, with a set of pedals for each rider. Powered by several people, such future cycles might be practical for all city transportation. People could form cycle pools instead of car pools to ride to and from work or school.

Another type of future cycle is also being tested—the skycycle. Skycycles are airplanes powered by pedals instead of engines. They are very light and have huge wings. So far, only athletes in top physical condition have

Plastic shells allow bicycles to go faster—up to 50 miles per hour. The riders of this tandem bicycle are competing in the International Human Powered Speed Championship.

This bicyclist also participated in the Human Powered Championship, an event held each year in Ontario, California.

been able to get skycycles off the ground. Cycles of this sort may never be practical, but engineers and cyclists in many countries are trying very hard to make them fly.

A more "down-to-earth" cycle of the future—and one that is already becoming very popular—is the moped. Part bicycle and part motorcycle, the moped is so named because it is a motorized bicycle complete with pedals. The first mopeds were made back in the 1890s, when engines were so weak and undependable that the pedals were a necessity. The mopeds of today are small, light, and fun to ride, with compact motors that can run for a long time on just a gallon of gas. They are inexpensive to buy, and they don't cost much to operate or maintain.

Mopeds are easy to ride and economical to operate.

Mopeds are easier and safer to operate than cars or motorcycles, and they don't make as much noise or cause as much pollution (most mopeds emit almost no noxious fumes). Mopeds can be operated with or without the engine because they have pedals. These pedals are used mainly to start the machines and to assist riders on hills. If the machines do run out of gas, however, the owners can simply pedal their way home.

These are only a few of the possibilities for future cycles. Some of them may well be the kinds of cycles people will be riding to work next year. Others may turn out to be dead ends, like the Macmillan cycle. What other ideas are there for future cycles? What do *you* think?

Superwheels & Thrill Sports

Lerner Publications Company
241 First Avenue North, Minneapolis, Minnesota 55401